25 APARTMENTS & LOFTS

UNDER 1000 SQUARE FEET

W9-BZT-425

25 APARTMENTS & LOFTS

UNDER 1000 SQUARE FEET

JAMES GRAYSON TRULOVE

COLLINS DESIGN

An Imprint of HarperCollinsPublishers

25 APARTMENTS UNDER 1000 SQUARE FEET

Copyright © 2008 by James Grayson Trulove and Collins Design

All rights reserved. No part of this book may be used or reproduced in any manner whatsoever without
written permission except in the case of brief quotations embodied in critical articles and reviews.
For information, address Collins Design, 10 East 53rd Street, New York, NY 10022.

HarperCollins books may be purchased for educational, business, or sales promotional use. For information, please write:
Special Markets Department, HarperCollins*Publishers,* 10 East 53rd Street, New York, NY 10022.

First published in 2008 by:
Collins Design
An Imprint of HarperCollins*Publishers*
10 East 53rd Street
New York, NY 10022
Tel: (212) 207-7000
Fax: (212) 207-7654
collinsdesign@harpercollins.com
www.harpercollins.com

Distributed throughout the world by:
HarperCollins*Publishers*
10 East 53rd Street
New York, NY 10022
Fax: (212) 207-7654

Packaged by:
Grayson Publishing, LLC
1250 28th Street NW
Washington, DC 20007
Tel: (202) 257-5959

Library of Congress Control Number: 2008922015

ISBN: 978-0-06-134020-8

Book Design by Agnieszka Stachowicz

Printed in China
First Printing, 2008

CONTENTS

FOREWORD

The idea of a cozy, small apartment tucked away in a vast urban forest has a broad and romantic appeal. Whether it be an escape from the suburbs for the weekend, or a permanent home, a small space, carefully planned, can provide for all of the creature comforts and more. As apartments presented in the book clearly demonstrate, fully equipped kitchens, spa-like bathrooms, opening entertaining spaces, and the ever popular home office are all possibilities. The key is to make the compact space do double, even triple duty throughout the day from eating, to sleeping, to working, to entertaining.

The project "Domestic Ribbon," serves as an excellent example of a carefully executed plan for a fully functioning living space in less than 400 square feet. By breaking with traditional notions of public and private space, the architect created one large open space tied together by a poured concrete "ribbon" that snakes through the apartment, defining spaces serving various functions throughout the apartment such as a bench or countertop or shower stall.

In another apartment, "Daydreams," a young couple, both of whom are architects, took a similar 400-square-foot space, and created an entirely different living environment. Because this is their full time residence, they successfully addressed issues such as accommodating overnight guests and the very practical need for ample storage.

Creating more efficient space or the illusion of more space can be equally challenging in larger apartments, especially when clients have long lists of requirements or when the basic, and often unchangeable layout of the apartment prevents easy solutions. However, there are solutions and the solutions that the architects and designers whose work is featured in 25 Apartments & Lofts Under 1000 Square Feet have come up with will provide the reader with a wealth of inspiration for overcoming challenges with their own compact apartment.

ABOVE: The pull down bed in the Domestic Ribbon apartment.
RIGHT: In the Lucentini apartment, a view of the kitchen from the living room. The walnut band serves to define the perimeter of the kitchen.

LEFT: White statuary marble was used for the walls and countertops in the 12th Street Apartment.
ABOVE: A detail of the rotating shelving unit in the 21st Street Apartment.
RIGHT: Leftover spaces in the master bathroom were converted into storage in the Two For One Apartment.

PROJECTS

DOMESTIC RIBBON

325 SQUARE FEET

ARCHITECT ALAN Y. L. CHAN • **PHOTOGRAPHERS** BRIAN RILEY, MICHEL FRIANG

This small apartment originally consisted of three separated rooms: the bathroom, the kitchen and the living room. These rooms were gloomy and confined with partitions blocking natural light between adjacent areas. To achieve a sense of openness and light in such a compact space, minimalist elements were inserted once the apartment was gutted. The flow of the new open plan is guided by the singular unifying element that encompasses all functions: a "domestic ribbon" of poured concrete. This ribbon unifies the space and as it elevates, descends, contracts, and expands, it serves to accommodate specific needs throughout the apartment.

The kitchen and bath are located adjacent to each other, separated by a plane of full height clear glass; a curtain behind the glass can be rolled down when privacy is desired. The interplay between the public and private, connected by the domestic ribbon element, stimulates an atmosphere of voyeurism and eroticism as functions become exposed.

Storage is essential in a small space, so in this apartment floor-to-ceiling carpentry runs the whole length of the living space along the side. On the other side of the ribbon is a sliding table that moves along the path enabling flexibility within the space. There are a number of elements within the apartment that serve dual functions, such as the light shelf that provides both illumination and shelving. A fabricated steel bench serves as a backsplash on the kitchen side and seating on the living and dining sides; and full height wall units have storage as well as a built-in pull down bed.

Floor Plan

PREVIOUS PAGE: The "domestic ribbon" moves through the kitchen, creating a bench and countertops.

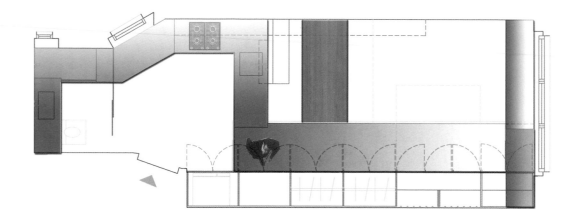

Ribbon Diagram

East Elevation, Cabinetry Closed

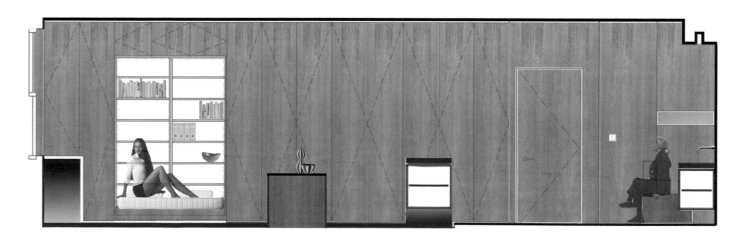

South Elevation

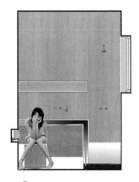

West Elevation

North Elevation

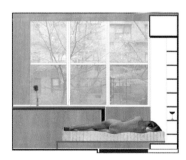

East Elevation, Cabinetry Opened

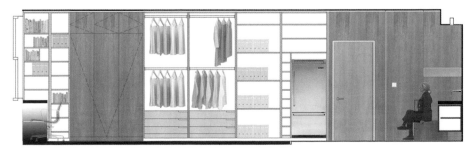

FAR LEFT AND LEFT: The pull down bed shown in the sleeping position and hidden. Exposed brick and unfinished plywood give the apartment a raw, urban feel.

LEFT: A view of the kitchen from the bathroom.
RIGHT: A fabricated steel bench serves as as backsplash for the kitchen sink.

LEFT: The bathroom is separated from the kitchen by a clear glass wall. A shade can be pulled down for privacy.

ABOVE AND ABOVE RIGHT: The domestic ribbon forms the vanity top and then dips to become the floor of the shower before rising again to become a bench.

LUCENTINI RESIDENCE

750 SQUARE FEET

ARCHITECT AB ARCHITECKTEN • **PHOTOGRAPHER** ARCHPHOTO

When creating a design for the remodeling of this Manhattan apartment, the architect utilized two built-in wooden elements to organize and reorient the space. The first element is a continuous three-dimensional walnut band that defines the perimeters of the relocated kitchen. The second element is a floating walnut plane that serves to define the transition between the living room and bedroom.

On an organizational level, several changes were made to the existing floor plan to optimize the use of space and to take advantage of the apartment's two exposures. First, the kitchen was moved into the previously oversized and underutilized hallway, freeing up space to create a large open living/dining area with windows providing north and south views of the city. Next, the bedroom was enlarged by extending it into the living area where a maple bookshelf separates the two rooms. The walnut plane above the bookshelf reconciles the offset in section created by this enlargement, preserving the symmetry of the ceiling structure as it relates to the living room window. When the sliding doors on either side of the bookshelf are retracted, the bookshelf becomes a functional island in a continuous living/sleeping area. In the bathroom the tub was relocated so that an additional door could be added to allow convenient access for guests to the bathroom without having to enter the bedroom.

Existing Floor Plan

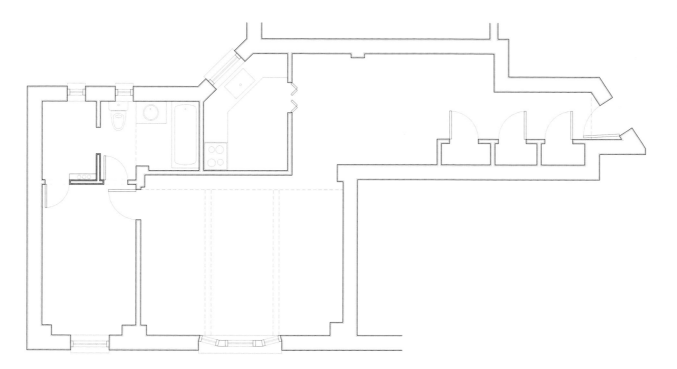

PREVIOUS PAGE: A view of the kitchen from the living room. The walnut band serves to define the perimeter of the kitchen.
RIGHT: The axonometric and sections detail the use of the wooden plane between the living room and bedroom and the wooden band that defines the kitchen area.

New Floor Plan

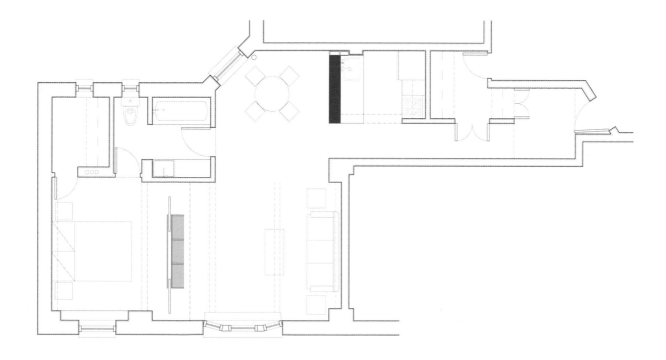

Axonometric

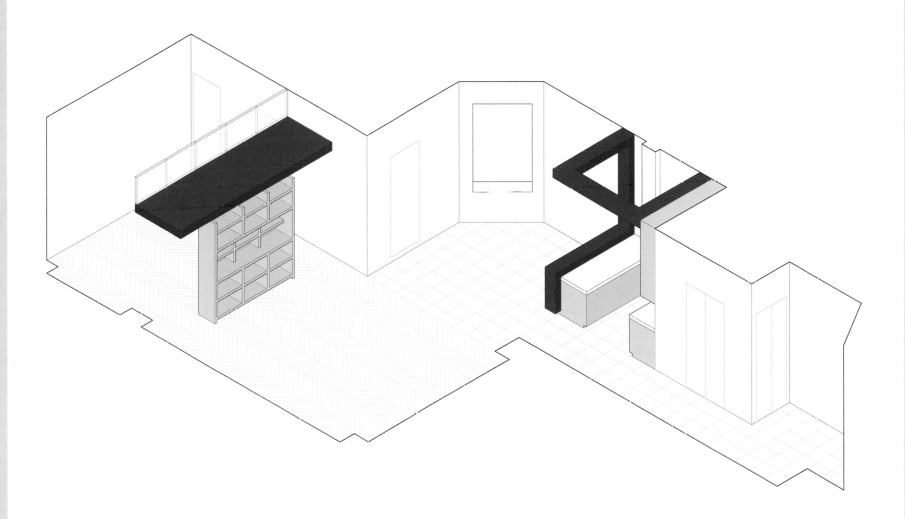

Sections

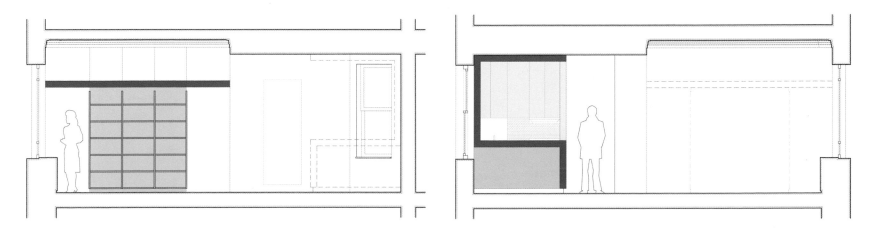

FAR LEFT: A view of the bookshelf separating the living room from the bedroom. Above the bookshelf is the floating wooden plane and above it is a clerestory window to bring additional light into the bedroom. By creating a space between the bookshelf and ceiling, both rooms are made to appear larger. Sliding glass doors are positioned on either side of the bookshelf.

LEFT: A door was added to the renovated bathroom to allow direct access to the living area for the convenience of guests.

HONG KONG APARTMENT

650 SQUARE FEET

ARCHITECT CHK DESIGN INSTITUTE • **PHOTOGRAPHER** CHK DESIGN INSTITUTE

In Hong Kong, perhaps one of the most densely populated cities in the world, every square foot of living space must be utilized, and in many cases, serve double duty. This apartment, owned by an international businessman who travels frequently to Hong Kong from Europe, is no exception. Envisioned as a tranquil space where the owner could recharge after long flights, the design is minimalist yet highly functional.

While compact, the apartment has been successfully divided into a public zone for modest entertaining, and a private zone for sleeping and work. Within this space, the bedroom area is separated by sliding glass doors, creating a quiet sanctuary. A work area at the end of this space enjoys views of the surrounding city.

Light colors and rich, natural woods and fabrics as well as strategically placed mirrors were used to finish the apartment, making it appear larger and more comfortable.

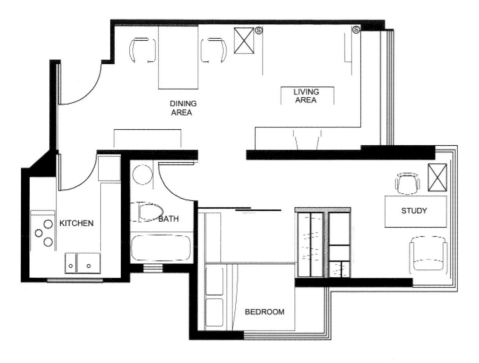

PREVIOUS PAGES: A view of the living and dining area as seen from the entry. The wall of windows is framed in a deep green, providing a strong contrast to the otherwise light color palette used in the apartment.

RIGHT: A media center separates the living area from the bedroom study area. Concealed lighting above and below the media wall is both dramatic and soothing.

FAR RIGHT: The study is placed in its own quiet corner with floor-to-ceiling windows overlooking the city. Furniture was carefully chosen that would not overwhelm the small apartment.

ABOVE: A view of the entry from the living area. A wall of mirrors at the entry creates the illusion of doubling the space. A mirror at the ceiling above the dining table also serves to visually expand the space.

RIGHT: A rich palette of wood and fabric create a tranquil environment for the bedroom.

ABOVE/BETWEEN LOFT

1000 SQUARE FEET

ARCHITECT ZERO PLUS • **PHOTOGRAPHER** ZERO PLUS

This addition and remodel of a condominium unit on the top floor of a turn of the century Georgian brick building began with making use of the attic that separated the unit from the roof. With an interest in investigating spatial relationships through prepositions: inhabitation above, upon, between, beneath, inside, beside, and through the attic, it transforms the existing space with the introduction, modification and combination of volumes. In its final form, the renovation resulted in a roof top terrace, a library loft, a shower skylight and a vaulted living room, each dynamically interacting with the existing spaces and drawing light from above deep into the unit.

The renovation was also a study in how juxtaposition between new and old relate to each to create a new coherent style. The new cabinetry in the kitchen is integrated into the original while not copying it exactly. In the living room, the new library art shelves and niche are carved into the existing attic and are exaggerated by adding to the original over-scaled crown molding. In the bathroom a complete transformation occurred referencing a recent trip to a Moroccan haman, although gauche bubbled limestone was substituted for the white marble of the haman. A new steel stair leads to the operable walk-through skylight to the roof deck and loft.

Attic Floor Plan

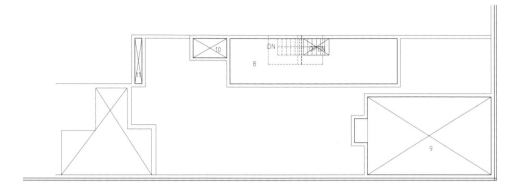

PREVIOUS PAGE: A view of the dining room and kitchen beyond from the living room. A library space was carved into the attic, framed by over-scaled crown molding.
RIGHT: A contemporary steel stair leads to the attic and the skylight to the roof terrace.
BELOW RIGHT: A detail of the skylight.
BELOW FAR RIGHT: The roof terrace.

Main Floor Plan

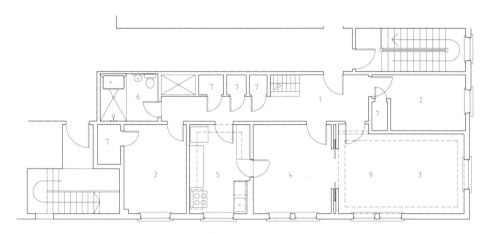

Section

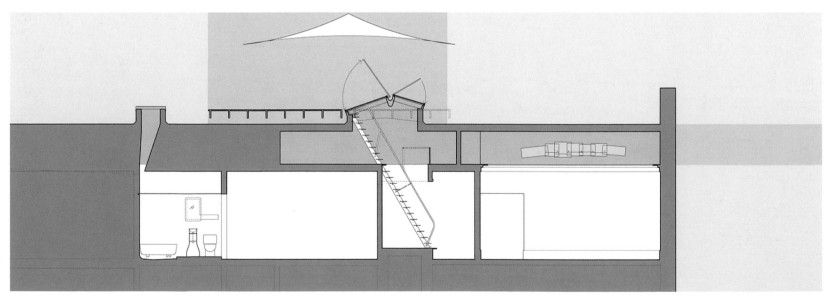

LEFT: The kitchen combines old and new.
TOP: The kitchen sink
ABOVE: The bathroom sink.
RIGHT: The shower receives natural light
from a new skylight.

KIMONO CABINET

840 SQUARE FEET

ARCHITECT ZERO PLUS • **PHOTOGRAPHER** BENJAMIN BENSCHNIEDER

This apartment is on the thirtieth floor of an early 1980's cast-in-place concrete high rise condominium building in downtown Seattle. The existing one-bedroom was stripped to its concrete shell and what the architects refer to as "the kimono cabinet" was installed in the middle of the unit. It was inspired by the client's interest in the efficiency of living simply and thus the concept—a giant tansu-like cabinet that holds everything—was the result. The bathroom, the kitchen, the laundry, and all the storage each unfolds from the cabinet when needed and folds away when not, letting uses overlap and accommodating all the activities of the day. A folding office is at the very end of the cabinet and completely disappears when not in use.

The floors in the apartment are limestone and the ceiling is the exposed cast-in-place concrete. The cabinet is painted and has exposed hardware. Panels of fabric laminated between sheets of glass create translucent areas. A set of steel shelves in the living room display art and a tall table anchored to the floor with steel pins doubles as an additional countertop and the dining room table.

Floor Plan

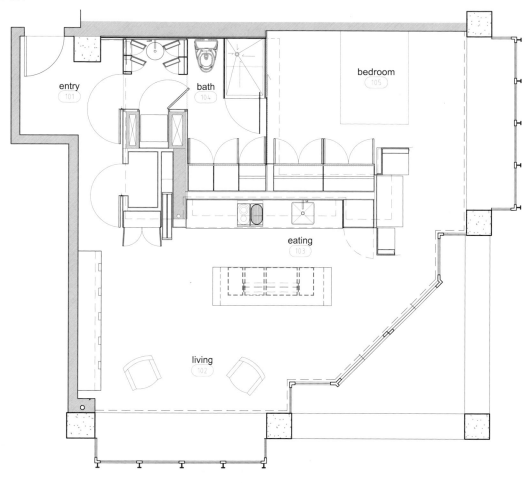

entry
101

bath
104

bedroom
105

eating
103

living
102

PREVIOUS PAGES (LEFT AND RIGHT):
A panoramic view of the cabinet with
all the compartments closed. A similar
view, showing the office on the end fully
opened and ready for use.
BELOW: Details of the cabinet hardware.
RIGHT: A tall table in the open kitchen
does double duty as a counter-top and
as the dining table.

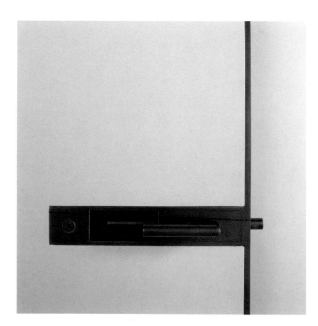

FAR LEFT: The cabinet frames the bedroom area.
LEFT: The bathroom is concealed within the cabinet.

GALLERY APARTMENT

990 SQUARE FEET

ARCHITECT DOMESTIC ARCHITECTURE • **PHOTOGRAPHER** MARK WOODS

This apartment was part of a larger scheme to adapt and reuse an existing warehouse building into a gallery that houses a private contemporary art collection. Within this larger space, the clients wanted to have a modest apartment that could serve several functions related to the operation of the gallery.

The apartment becomes an entertaining space for intimate gatherings at the gallery, For larger events, it functions as a commercial kitchen and food preparation area, and it serves as a residence for visiting artists while creating commissioned work for the gallery. In addition, the apartment is an important part of the exhibition space for the larger gallery and is generally open to the public during gallery hours.

The gallery and apartment's lead designer, Roy McMakin, is an artist himself, and he conceived of the overall space as a sculptural installation. Each part of the building, including the apartment, works together to form a whole.

Section

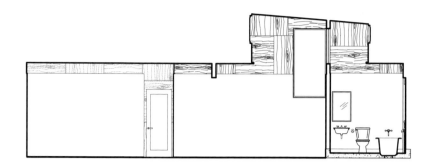

PREVIOUS PAGES: A view of the living area from the kitchen. Exposed ceiling joists and steel structural components give the space a raw, loft-like quality.
RIGHT: A view from the living area to the open kitchen.
BELOW: Entry.

Floor Plan

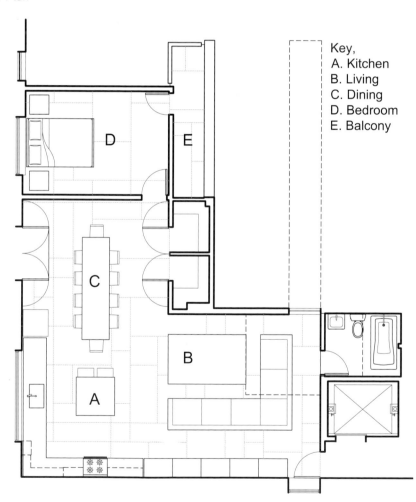

Key,
A. Kitchen
B. Living
C. Dining
D. Bedroom
E. Balcony

FAR LEFT AND LEFT: The commerical-grade kitchen is used for large-scale food preparation when there is an exhibit opening at the gallery.

BROOKLYN APARTMENT

600 SQUARE FEET

ARCHITECT ROBERT KANER INTERIOR DESIGN • **PHOTOGRAPHER** TOM POWEL IMAGING

Although only 600 square feet, the renovation of this apartment resulted in significant storage space, a niche for a home office, and ample living space. A color palette and clean modern details were introduced to visually open up the space. A medium-dark hardwood floor is in contrast to the off-white walls and the bright white ceiling. Soft colors are used along one wall in each room to provide a visual anchor. Closet doors in the hallway and bedroom have flush pivot-hinges with minimal hardware, allowing them to blend with surrounding walls and create more unified surfaces.

The entry hallway is multifunctional. Besides providing for circulation among the various areas of the apartment, it contains a niche at one end for a built-in home office unit and opposite the entry door is a bank of floating shelving providing a visual pull into the apartment from the entrance.

The small bathroom was expanded visually. As in the rest of the apartment, a relatively dark floor is used to ground the space. The pattern of wall tiles creates a sense of openness, transitioning from a darker color concentration at the bottom to a lighter, modulated color concentration at eye level and above, leading to the bright white ceiling. The shower area has been incorporated visually into the bathroom, with the room's perimeter walls continuing uninterrupted into the shower. A frameless glass partition enhances this visual connection. A large recessed medicine cabinet with mirrored doors visually expands the room while providing additional storage space. More storage is introduced through stone niches in one of the shower walls, and from a new floor-to-ceiling closet taken in part from an adjacent hallway closet, with a fully tiled concealed door that blends with the walls.

Floor Plan

BEDROOM

LIVING ROOM

BATH

HALLWAY

KITCHEN

OFFICE

PREVIOUS PAGES: To contrast with the all off-white apartment, one wall in each room is painted a different, soft color.

ABOVE: A medium-dark wood parquet floor running throughout the apartment visually connects the rooms.

ABOVE: An open bookcase was installed opposite the entry door. It acts as a focal point upon entering the apartment while providing additional storage.

LEFT: Also in the entry hallway is a niche containing a fully equipped home office.

FAR LEFT: The window wall of the bedroom is painted a light pastel. LEFT AND ABOVE: Several clever design touches were employed to make the small bathroom appear larger. The wall tiles become lighter towards the ceiling; the tiled walls continue into the shower stall, creating a visual continuum; and a clear glass shower door and large vanity mirror visually expand the space.

PLAYERS PAD

1000
SQUARE FEET

ARCHITECT RB ARCHITECTS • **PHOTOGRAPHER** JAMES WILKINS

The center of the social space in this renovated one-bedroom apartment is the dining area. It has a suspended ceiling, which houses a light cove that continues along the wall, allowing the lighting to be adjusted to set the mood for any occasion. The dining area opens on one side to a kitchen with stainless steel and black wood veneer cabinets, and absolute black stone countertop and backsplash. On the other side is the living area, with spectacular views of New York and the East River.

White lacquer and opal glass sliding doors and white lacquer cabinetry define the den, with its entertainment center and television. In the master bedroom, a custom platform bed/canopy, also with a hidden light cove, is made of zebrano and black wood veneers, which is also used for a wall that conceals the doors to the walk-in closet and bathroom. In the guest and master bathrooms, black and white ceramic tile, glass, and stone continue the apartment's muted palette.

Floor Plan

PREVIOUS PAGES: Sliding doors
with frosted glass separate the
living area from the den.
RIGHT: A light cove in the ceiling
continues down the wall of the
dining room.
FAR RIGHT: Behind the dining
area is a wall of closets separating
it from the guest bathroom.

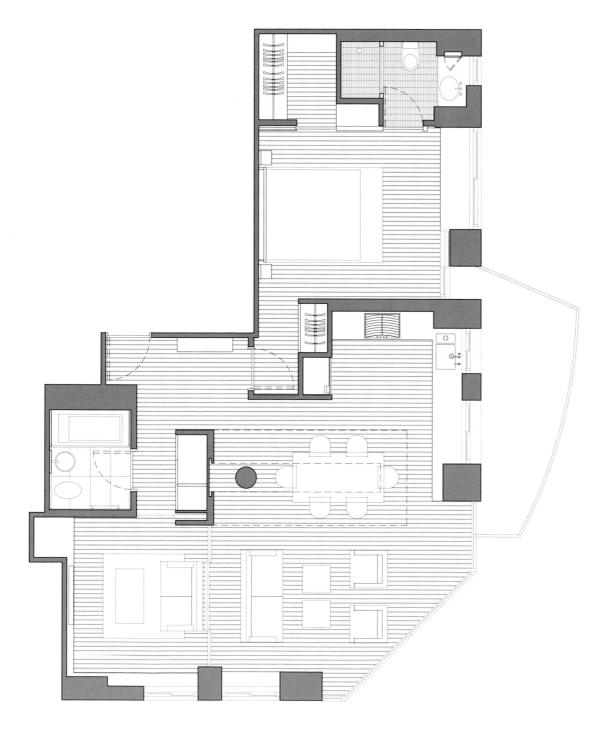

RIGHT AND ABOVE: The dining area overlooks the sleek, modern kitchen that is equipped with stainless steel and black veneer cabinetry.

LEFT AND ABOVE: Mahogany cabinetry
and Absolute black granite finishes
the kitchen. The floors throughout the
apartment are bamboo.

LEFT: A custom wood canopy over the bed acts as a light cove.
ABOVE: The same dark wood is used for the bed's platform and for the the closet doors.

ABOVE: The guest bathroom
RIGHT: The master bathroom

CHELSEA APARTMENT

575 SQUARE FEET

ARCHITECT RB ARCHITECTS • **PHOTOGRAPHER** JAMES WILKINS

As with most small apartments, the need for flexibility and privacy drove the renovation of this project. Existing walls were replaced with full height movable panels made of unfinished laminated plywood. These panels are located at each side of a fixed, gray plaster wall that acts as the hub of the apartment. The movable panels provide privacy for the bathroom on one side and for the office and bedroom on the other. In addition, full height mirror doors on the living area closet create reflected views and bring light in the apartment.

The kitchen was renovated with white plastic laminate cabinets and stainless steel countertop and backsplash, as well as new stainless steel appliances. A new home office alcove was located where a closet used to be. It is made out of birch plywood with a clear coat finish.

In the bedroom a new closet was designed with full height ultrasuede panels framed with aluminum. A custom designed platform bed frame using full height walnut veneer plywood panels with concealed bookcase/shelving space behind continues the emphasis on the vertical planes. A finished plaster was used for the wall.

The use of the full height panels instead of traditional doors reduces visual clutter and emphasizes the verticality of the space, making it seem larger and more open.

Floor Plan

PREVIOUS PAGES: A low multi-functional bookcase separates the living area from the kitchen. It is constructed of the same white plastic laminate as the kitchen cabinets.
RIGHT: Unfinished floor-to-ceiling plywood panels close to provide privacy for the bathroom and dressing areas from the living and dining areas.

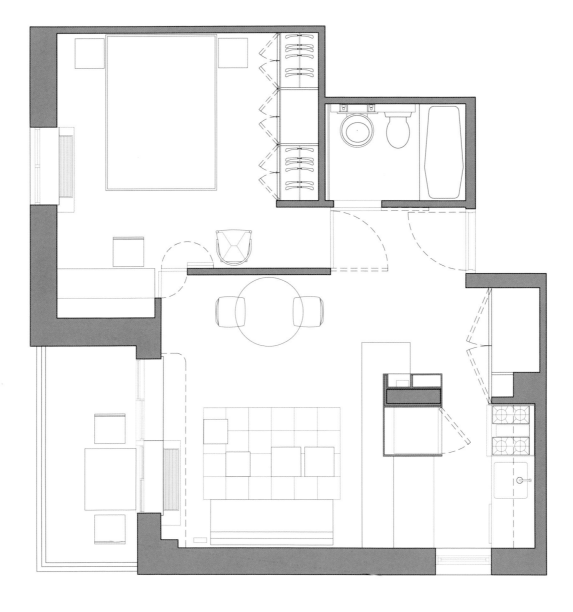

LEFT: Mirrored closet doors provide added depth to the space and bring in needed light. RIGHT: A bedroom closet was converted into a home office work area.

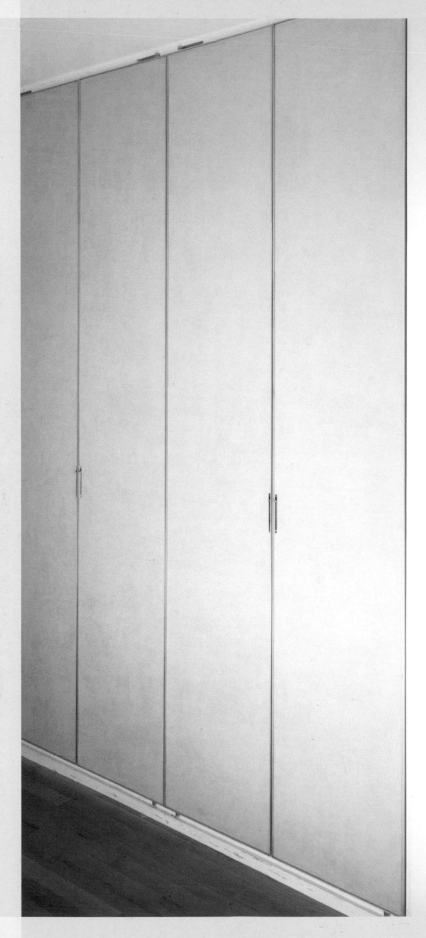

LEFT: A view of the sliding plywood panels that separate the living area from the bedroom. A new closet was constructed using full height ultrasuede panels framed with aluminum.

RIGHT: The bed was custom designed with shelving concealed behind walnut veneer panels.

ARRIGHI APARTMENT

900 SQUARE FEET

ARCHITECT CARL SHENTON • **PHOTOGRAPHER** EDUARD HUEBER/ARCHPHOTO

The project involved a gut renovation including the replacement of the windows and the installation of a split air-conditioning system. The original ceilings, over eleven feet high, were restored to expose the beam structure that helped to define the organization of the new apartment layout. In order to maximize natural light and open up views from the apartment, the layout is divided into three layers from enclosed to semi-open to open. The bedroom is set back as far as possible within the central section so that the living room can occupy the entire width of the window wall.

Every effort was made to design a space that could be used as efficiently as possible. The bedroom is a flexible space that can be completely open to the living room and kitchen during the day, creating one large area. This is achieved with sliding and folding glass doors on two sides of the bedroom that can be partially or completely opened. The glass is etched to provide privacy to the bedroom, which also creates a diffuse lighting effect to the living and kitchen areas at night.

The open plan kitchen features a long island that acts as a food preparation area, and it can be extended to create a dining table that projects into the living room. Three pendant lamps over the island mark this area as a focal point with warm light.

The finishing materials are a simple palette of glass, metal, stone and American walnut. The glass bedroom doors and living room windows are framed in anodized aluminum while the kitchen island, appliances and backsplash are in brushed stainless steel. The bathroom floor and walls are tiled in limestone and the kitchen countertops use Italian sandstone.

Floor Plan

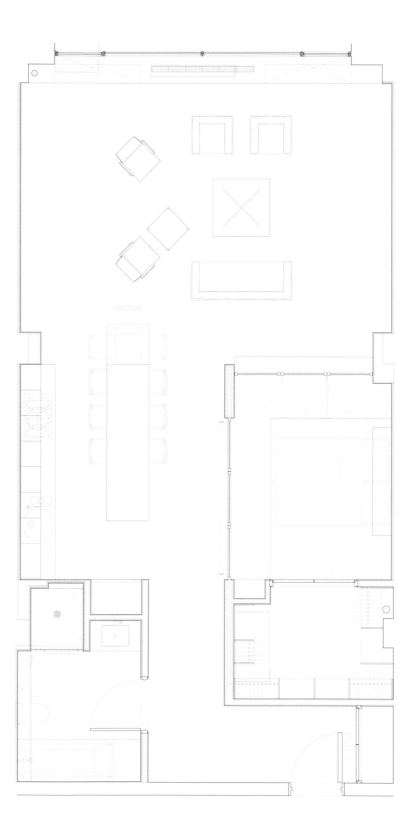

PREVIOUS PAGES: An evening view from the kitchen, across the kitchen island to the living room. The bedroom is to the right. With all the sliding glass doors open, the apartment becomes one large living area.

RIGHT: A view from the living area to the kitchen and bedroom with the etched glass doors separating the bedroom in the open position. The stainless steel kitchen island is shown in its folded position.

FAR LEFT: A view of the sliding glass doors of the bedroom in the closed position. When closed, the etched glass provides privacy while allowing diffused light to enter the bedroom.

LEFT: The stainless steel kitchen island is shown in its extended position in order to provide additional seating.

LEFT: With the glass doors open, the bedroom becomes an integral part of the apartment.

ABOVE: With the doors closed, it becomes a private space, well-lit by natural light during the day.

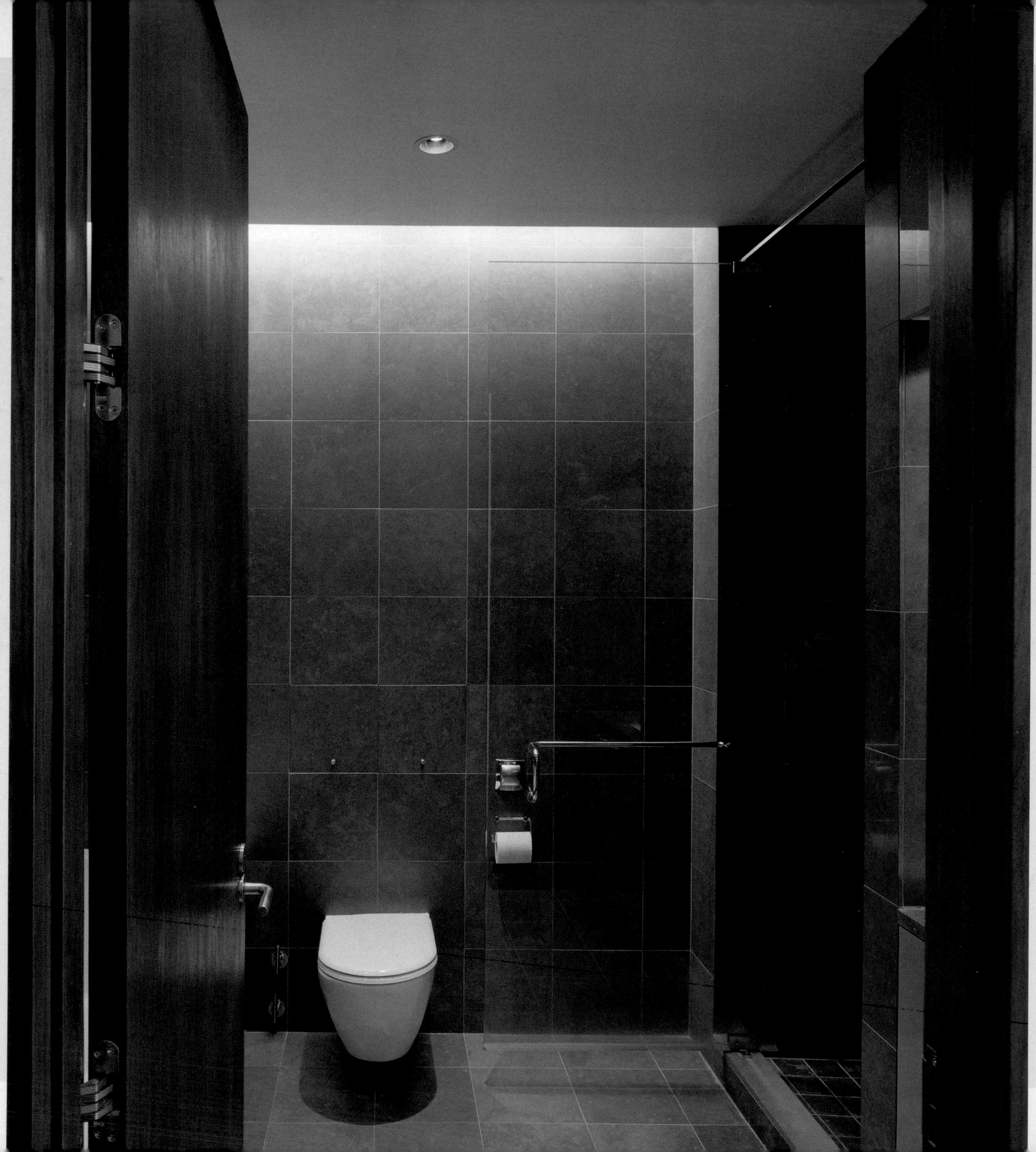

LEFT AND RIGHT: The bathroom acts as a counterpoint to the light, open plan design of the rest of the apartment, with a sense of luxury provided by the finishes, the generous shower and bath and three separate lighting systems that can be used together or individually to define the mood of the space.

MALINA LOFT

875 SQUARE FEET

ARCHITECT MAS MANIFOLD ARCHITECTURE STUDIO • **PHOTOGRAPHER** EDUARD HUEBER/ARCHPHOTO

The challenge for the architect of this project was to maintain the desired elements of the existing loft such as high ceilings and an open, flexible plan while creating distinct, functional areas that could be transformed as necessary. He began by reconfiguring the existing bathroom and kitchen layout, bringing the kitchen forward into the living space, which then allowed the bathroom to expand and occupy the previous kitchenette area, doubling in size.

The owners of the apartment needed sufficient workspace for two with the option to hide the work area when necessary. There was also a large library of books to consider. These two requirements were configured together as a continuous element along the east wall of the apartment, creating a new floor-to-ceiling wall filled with books on the side near the dining area that folds into a wall of enclosed shelf units and desk space.

Another challenge was to define a sleeping area without diminishing the openness of the loft. Fortunately there was an area towards the rear of the loft that provided the most privacy as well as access to a large closet. A wall was built with 30-inch-wide floor-to-ceiling pocket doors on both sides. When the doors are open, this wall acts as a backdrop for the living area rather than a solid enclosure.

Floor Plan

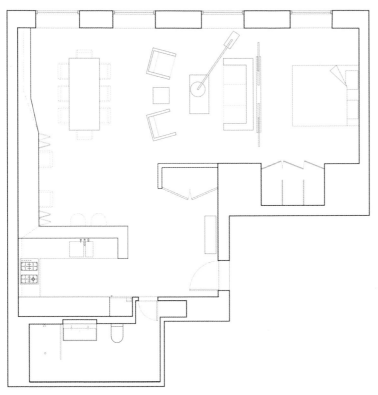

PREVIOUS PAGES: A two-person workspace across one wall of the loft is located in the area that also functions as a dining room. The workstations can be closed when not in use.

RIGHT: A view of the bookcase as seen from along the window-wall of the loft.

FAR RIGHT: A view to the living area from the kitchen.

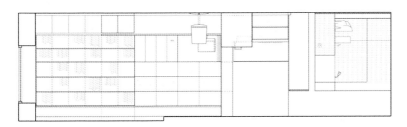

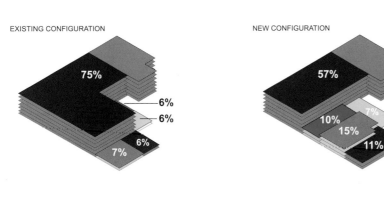

EXISTING CONFIGURATION

75%

6%

6%

6%

7%

NEW CONFIGURATION

57%

7%

10%

15%

11%

◆ Living/Bedroom   ◆ Kitchen   ◇ Entrance Area
Home Office   Bathroom

LEFT: The minimalist kitchen opens onto the living/dining/ work area. The bathroom is located behind the kitchen. The location of the two were flipped during the renovation.
RIGHT: The appliances are hidden within the well-crafted cabinetry.

LEFT AND RIGHT: A generously-sized bathroom is made to seem even larger and brighter through the use of glass wall tiles, a glass shower enclosure and a large mirror.

ROOFTOP APARTMENT

960 SQUARE FEET

ARCHITECT MCINTURFF ARCHITECTS • **PHOTOGRAPHER** JULIA HEINE

This rooftop apartment is one of six units above an historic building in the Georgetown neighborhood of Washington D.C.. It sits squarely in the center of a new roof garden that provides a quiet oasis high above the city.

The two-story apartment has a master bedroom suite and the main entry located on the first floor. An oak stairway leads to the upper floor, which is one large open room to take advantage of south-facing views over the city. Here are located the living, dining and kitchen areas.

Downstairs, outdoor space is provided by a small private garden that enlarges the bedroom, while upstairs a balcony extends the width of the living room. Ample windows open both levels to the south, while smaller windows to the sides and north allow for views, privacy, and ventilation.

Throughout, simple light materials are used to create a luminous interior for this rooftop sanctuary.

Floor Plans

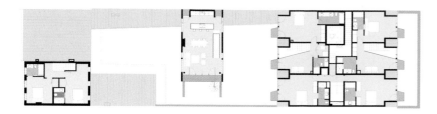

PREVIOUS PAGES: The stairway leads from the entry level below to the open living, dining and kitchen areas above. A balcony extends the width of the space for outdoor entertaining.

RIGHT: A view of the kitchen area from the living area. The kitchen is framed in smaller windows at the rear and on the sides.

Computer Model

LEFT: A private garden extends off the glass-walled master bedroom.

21ST STREET APARTMENT

850 SQUARE FEET

ARCHITECT PULLTAB • **PHOTOGRAPHER** ELIZABETH FELICELLA

This apartment is in a building that was erected in 1905, and during this renovation, many original architectural elements were discovered, hidden beneath layers of previous renovations. Period moldings, door casings, glass transoms, plaster crowns, glazed tiles and door hardware were researched and restored. However, an open plan was created through the removal of dark and confining compartmentalized rooms in order to create a more modern, livable apartment.

The main living space includes the kitchen, dining and living areas. Hand selected granite countertops were used to connect these spaces and to complement the restored glazed tile fireplace surround. To maximize storage, a premium in city apartments, a hidden closet was created by installing a rotating shelving unit in an inactive dumbwaiter shaft in the living room.

New Douglas fir two-and-one-quarter-inch wood flooring was installed throughout the apartment. One hundred-year-old glass knob passage door hardware and bathroom accessories were found in an architectural salvage yard to create an authentic period appearance.

By the respectful blending of modern "insertions" and the restoration of period detailing this Chelsea renovation balances the desire to live in a modern space while being grounded in a turn of the century building.

Floor Plan

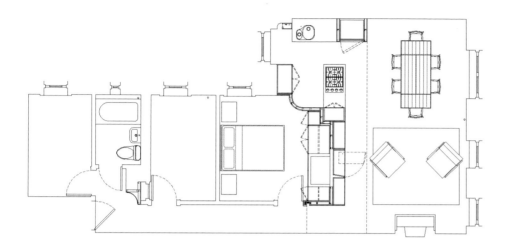

0 1 2 6

PREVIOUS PAGES: A view of the
open kitchen from the dining area.
RIGHT: A detail of the rotating shelving unit that was fashioned within
the shaft of an unused
dumbwaiter.
BELOW: The glazed tile surround
on the existing fireplace mantel was
restored. The granite countertops
in the kitchen were selected to
complement this tile. The traditional
moldings on the mantel are a pleasing
contrast with the modern furniture.

Bookshelf Axonometric

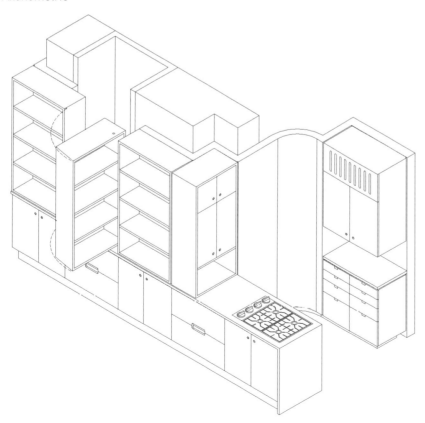

LEFT AND RIGHT: The bookshelf unit separates the living and dining areas from the bedroom behind. The architects attempted to give the apartment a modern feeling while being respectful of its original architectural details.

ABOVE: A view from the entry corridor toward the living area.

RIGHT: A view from the bedroom into the corridor. The floors are Douglas fir and doors and hardware provide period details.

ABOVE: Soap holder detail.
LEFT: A view of the remodeled bathroom.

PENTHOUSE OASIS

300 SQUARE FEET

ARCHITECT PULLTAB • **PHOTOGRAPHER** ELIZABETH FELICELLA

Designed as a space for both reading and entertaining, the East Village Penthouse is part of a larger private residence located on the top floor of an early 1900's Manhattan walkup. The architects were retained to design a series of renovations to a loft space along with a new penthouse and garden area atop an existing roof, accessed through the fifth floor loft.

In creating the indoor/outdoor space, a palette of materials (teak, bronze, zinc and Cor-ten steel) was selected allowing the design to season through cycles of weathering.

For durability, the solid teak windows, doors and columns were assembled using traditional joinery details, inspired by the techniques of wooden boat building. Exterior teak screens, set within the window mullion system, form a brise-soleil.

Inside the space, a series of three teak cruciform columns carry part of the roof load. These columns are constructed with dado joints and mechanically fastened with silicon bronze screws. In the method of fine furniture building, no glue has been used in their assembly.

Set within a hand assembled galvanized standing seam metal roof, a custom steel plate water trough is welded to a load bearing structural steel tube. The trough and beam act together, creating a composite section which forms a "spine" for the teak rafters and also a collection and dispersion device for rainwater.

Floor Plan

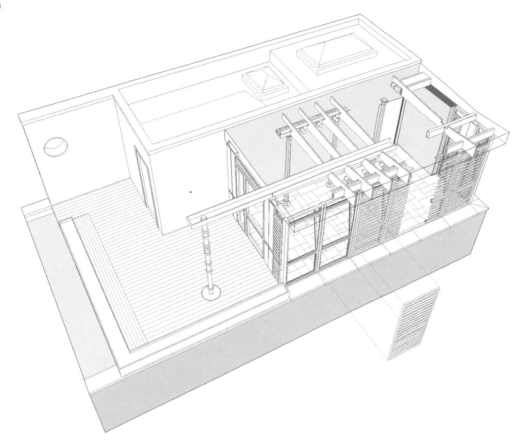

PREVIOUS PAGE: Designed as a living environment for all seasons, the penthouse allows for a reprieve from the city, while still connecting the owner to the surrounding cityscape. ABOVE: Privacy screens are constructed of Cor-ten steel.

Model

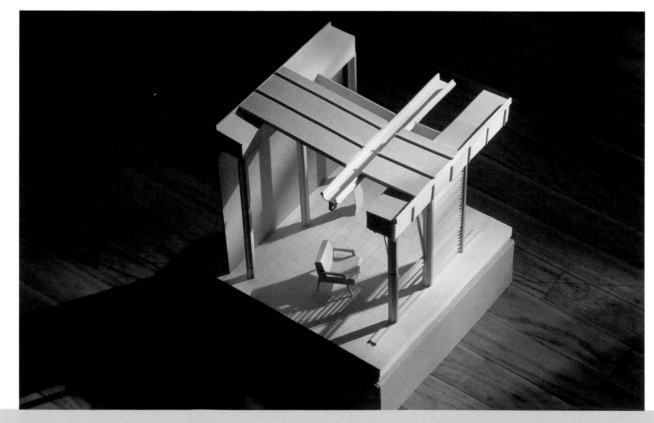

ABOVE: Flowing into the zinc lined steel trough the collected rainwater makes its way through a cantilevered section, continuing down the outside of a weathered steel post. The water then passes through a bronze ring, placed in the teak deck, and on to the existing roof. Adjustable zinc plated discs are mounted on the weathered steel post. Recessed set screws allow the owner to loosen these discs and slide them up and down, "tuning" the waterfall.

FAR LEFT AND LEFT: Inside, the screens create both a sun block, for the higher angle of the summer sun, and also a device to note the passing time. As the sun tracks across the sky, the horizontal slats broadcast a continually changing pattern of light and shadow.

ABOVE AND RIGHT: Interior roof detail.

EMPTY NESTER APARTMENT

900 SQUARE FEET

ARCHITECT GHISLAINE VINAS DESIGN • **PHOTOGRAPHER** ELIZABETH FELICELLA

This apartment was renovated to accommodate empty nesters moving from the suburbs into the city to reinvent their lives now that their children are grown. When they bought their apartment it was in need of updating, particularly the kitchen and bathrooms. The cramped kitchen was opened up to the dining and living areas, creating a brighter, more engaging space. A muted color palette and minimalist cabinetry are in harmony with the spare, modern aesthetic that the designers chose to give the entire apartment. The new maple floors further contribute to the crisp, clean look of the apartment.

Both bathrooms were gutted and contemporary fixtures and glass tiles give the bathrooms new life and make them compatible with the design of the rest of the apartment.

The master bedroom was outfitted with built-ins around the radiator and given clean, crisp new closet doors. The second bedroom serves as an office and also has built-ins and a desk around the radiators. It has a folding bed so that when the couple's children come home from college for the weekend, the office quickly converts back to a bedroom.

PREVIOUS PAGES: The kitchen was opened up to the living and dining areas, creating a brighter, more functional space. Maple was chosen for the floors, in keeping with the modern aesthetic chosen by the designers.
ABOVE: New cabinetry and stainless steel appliances give the kitchen a crisp, modern feel.
RIGHT: Additional storage space is hidden behind sliding frosted mirror glass doors.

LEFT: A view from the dining area into the open kitchen. A dramatic contemporary lighting fixture defines the dining area.

RIGHT: The second bedroom serves as a spacious office or a sleeping area, thanks to the folding bed.

ABOVE AND LEFT: Both bathrooms were renovated using contemporary fixtures and tiles.
RIGHT: The master bedroom.

12TH STREET APARTMENT

825 SQUARE FEET

ARCHITECT MESSANA O'RORKE ARCHITECTS • **PHOTOGRAPHER** ELIZABETH FELICELLA

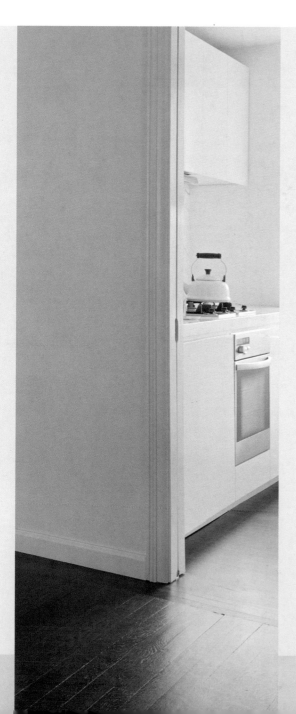

The entry to the apartment overlooks a sunken living room and fireplace where two continuous steps run the length of the room. The original exposed brick fireplace was encased in sheetrock and given a new black slate hearth. Window and base moldings were removed or replaced throughout the apartment and the floors were refinished with an ebony stain.

Opposite the front door, the kitchen has an etched glass pocket door to bring daylight into the entry area. The ebony floors continue into the galley kitchen which has an undercounter refrigerator to maximize the counter space. The cabinets and appliance panels are finished in white lacquer and the countertops and walls are finished in white statuary marble.

A single slab of white statuary marble was cut into four segments to form the floor of the new shower room, the walls of this room were refinished in white ceramic tiles and a fixed sheet of clear glass divides the shower from the space. The bedroom has a library built behind white lacquer doors opposite the window.

Floor Plan

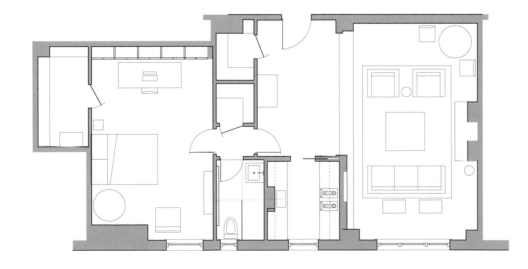

PREVIOUS PAGE: The sunken living room as viewed from the entry, with the galley kitchen to the right.
ABOVE LEFT: A view of the etched glass kitchen door from the entry.
ABOVE AND RIGHT: The kitchen countertops and walls are finished in white statuary marble.

LEFT: The bathroom is finished in white ceramic tile and white statuary marble.
RIGHT: A view to the entry from the master bedroom.

FLEXIBLE SPACE

975 SQUARE FEET

ARCHITECT MESSANA O'RORKE ARCHITECTS • **PHOTOGRAPHER** ELIZABETH FELICELLA

This apartment is centred around the design of a single storage wall that divides public from private space. The storage wall separates the master bedroom from the living room and the guest room from the kitchen. The wall can be circumnavigated through a third pocket door between the master bedroom closet and the guest room. The wall has twelve-foot-tall translucent plastic and poplar pocket doors that allow each area of the apartment to blend with the other when the doors are open.

At the entry to the apartment, the hall closet and shower room are hidden behind a wall of white lacquer panels. An existing concrete column defines the entry hall from the living room beyond. The living room centers on an existing fireplace, which is also visible from the master bedroom when the pocket door is open. The adjacent, open kitchen is finished in white Corian and walnut.

The master bathroom is finished in limestone, Venetian plaster and glass tile, undermount white porcelain sinks reflect the undermount tub which is similarly embedded in a limestone platform.

The entire apartment is enlivened by a series of exposed and obscured dimmable fluorescent light fixtures, which bring bright daylight-quality light into its darkest recesses.

PREVIOUS PAGES: A view of the living area from the open kitchen.
LEFT: A walnut wall defines and adds warmth to the kitchen. One of the translucent pocket doors in the storage wall is visible on the right.
RIGHT: The living room as seen from one of the bedrooms. When the pocket doors are open, the apartment becomes more open and loft-like.

Floor Plan

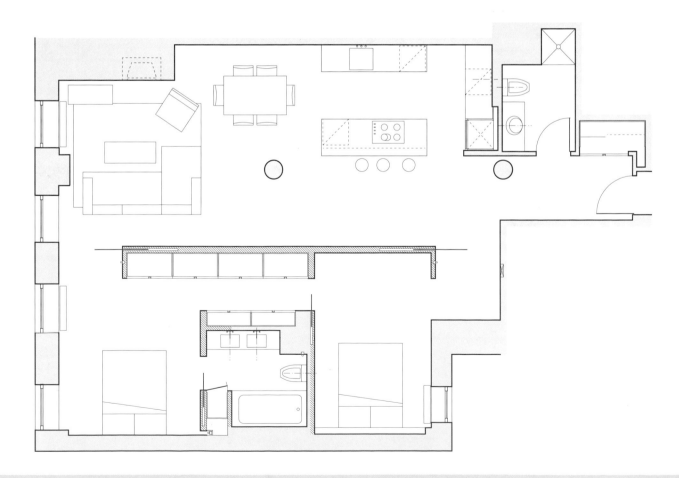

LEFT AND BELOW: Limestone, Venetian plaster and glass tile were used to create a simple and clear bathroom design.
RIGHT: A view of the bedroom through the open translucent pocket door.

DORSINVILLE LOFT

520 SQUARE FEET

ARCHITECT MESSANA O'RORKE ARCHITECTS • **PHOTOGRAPHER** ELIZABETH FELICELLA

The architects' conceived of the design for this apartment as a mini loft with the bedroom, living room and shower room combined as one space. A teak room divider containing storage and electronic equipment became the nexus among these three functional areas. The large south facing window marries the living room and sleeping area but neither has direct visual contact with the other. A single white lacquer window sill storage cabinet further enhances the perception of unlimited space. An acid etched glass panel slides into the teak cabinet as the door from the living space. Curtained floor to ceiling clear glass divides the sleeping area from the bathroom, so that with the curtain open the view over the city can be enjoyed from inside the shower.

The ceiling is a continuous plan floating over the teak room divider, washed by up lighting from below. The teak cabinet appears to float over the floor thanks to a lighting strip underneath it. Foldaway doors make it possible to operate and watch the television from both the living room and bedroom side of the room divider. The bed is raised off the floor on a custom ashe platform, which forms a shelf in an alcove either side of the mattress.

PREVIOUS PAGES:A teak room divider appears to float between the living and sleeping areas of the apartment.
RIGHT: The divider provides storage and houses electronic equipment.
FAR RIGHT: White lacquer panels and doors start at the foyer, providing additional storage and visually unifying the design of the apartment.

FAR LEFT: The kitchen, which is adjacent to the foyer, was extended into a broom closet and refitted with ashen and stainless steel cabinetry and under counter appliances.

LEFT: The former coat closet was converted into a home office.

ABOVE: A view of the bedroom from the living room.
RIGHT: Floor-to-ceiling clear glass divides the sleeping area from the bathroom. Curtains provide privacy but can be opened to provide a view of the city from the shower.

STOREFRONT LOFT

1000 SQUARE FEET

ARCHITECT MESSANA O'RORKE ARCHITECTS • **PHOTOGRAPHER** ELIZABETH FELICELLA

This clean, modern loft was fashioned from a storefront in the East Village of Manhattan. While the space required a complete remodeling, it nevertheless had twelve-foot ceilings, steel columns and thick wooden beams that the architects used to create a dramatic interior living space. A wall of opaque plastic simulates sunshine opposite the entry hall. The apartment is entered through a square arch that opens into the living area that has a high-level slot window, which provides views of the sky to the south. The kitchen is finished in white lacquer and stainless steel.

A linear light fixture runs the length of the space, passing from the large gallery-type space through a narrow gap between enclosed spaces into another space beyond. Each area is defined by architecture, but function is abstracted, hidden and obscured. A sofa, a table, or a bed becomes the only element that describes the domestic function of each space.

Floor Plan

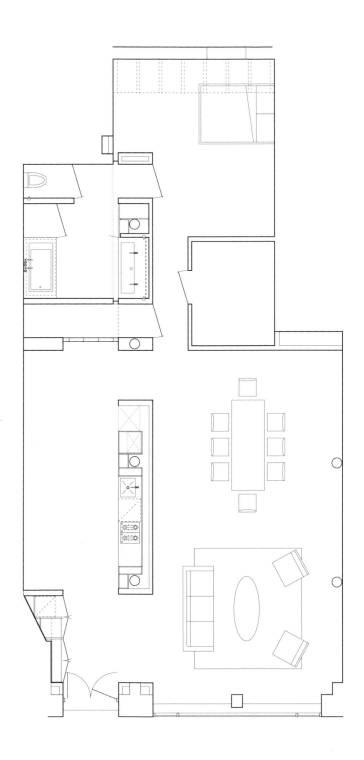

PREVIOUS PAGE: A view from the dining area toward the front of the apartment, which is at street level. BELOW: A view of the living area from the entry. The linear lighting fixture that runs the length of the apartment is visible at the top. RIGHT: A view from the living area to the entry.

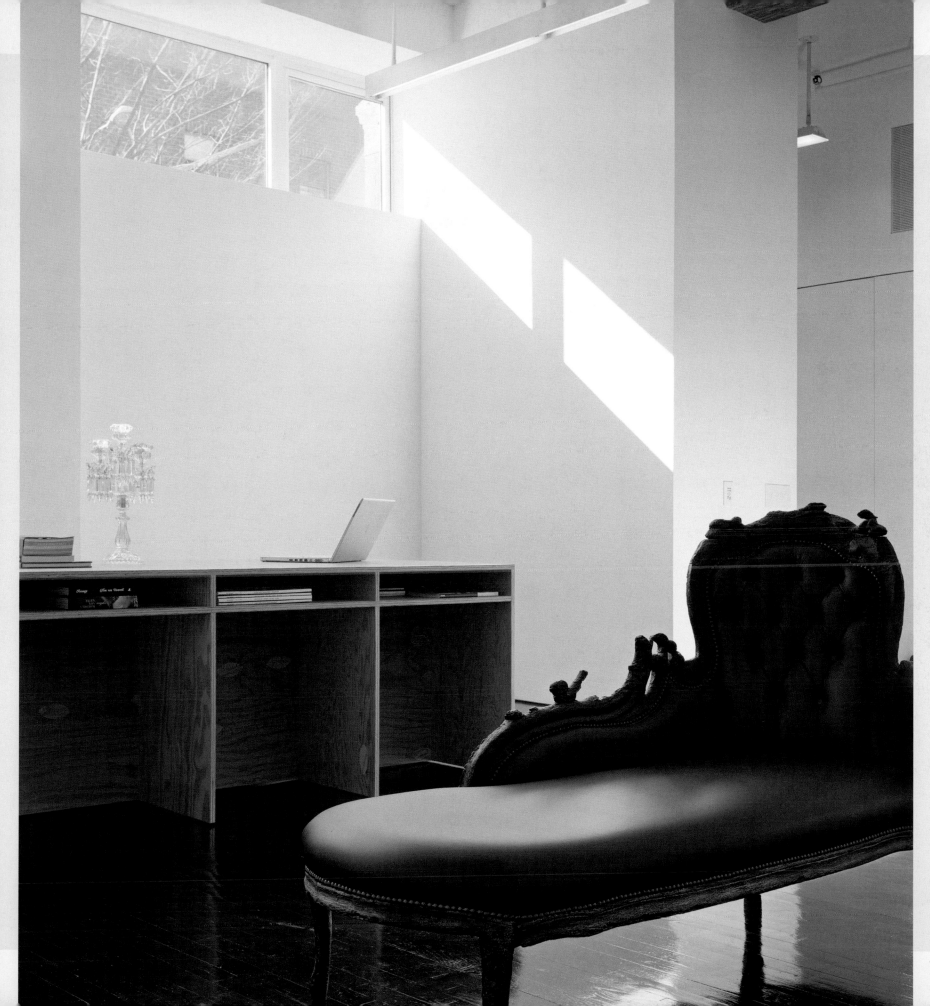

LEFT: The simple, modern kitchen is finished in white lacquer with stainless steel appliances.
RIGHT: A view from the kitchen back to the entry.

LEFT: Existing wooden beams were left exposed, their coarseness contrasting with the apartment's smooth white surfaces.
RIGHT: Translucent sliding glass doors provide privacy while bringing light into the bedroom.

RIGHT AND FAR RIGHT: The generous spa-like bathroom continues the clean, minimalist theme used throughout the storefront loft.

TWO FOR ONE APARTMENT

920 SQUARE FEET

ARCHITECT IAIN CAMPBELL DESIGN • **PHOTOGRAPHER** CHRISTOPHER CAMPBELL

By combining two small studio apartments, the architect was able to create a comfortable one-bedroom for his client. One studio was converted into a bedroom with a small home office, and generously proportioned bath and dressing room. The second studio became an informal open space with a living room, eat-in kitchen and a powder room.

By removing the tub, and relocating the sink from the original bathroom, a longer, more open kitchen was made possible. The kitchen is fitted with custom cabinets and stainless steel countertops. The stainless steel oval base to the island hides storage.

In the master bath, the walls were rebuilt and tiled in stone. A former closet was turned into a generous shower room. The second kitchen became a storage closet and home office while a sleeping alcove became a media niche opening onto the living room.

In the bedroom, the bed and shelving units were custom designed by the architect and were made to look as though they were "floating" on the wall.

Existing Floor Plan

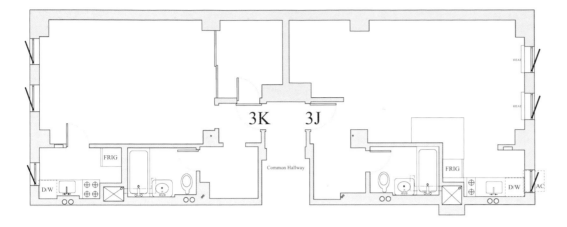

3K   3J

New Floor Plan

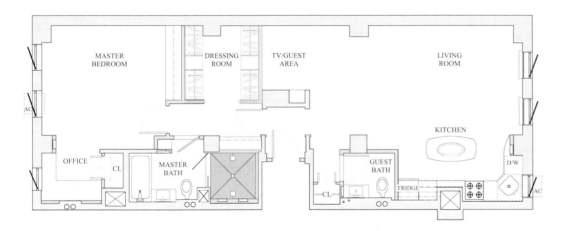

MASTER
BEDROOM

DRESSING
ROOM

TV/GUEST
AREA

LIVING
ROOM

KITCHEN

OFFICE

CL

MASTER
BATH

GUEST
BATH

CL

FRIDGE

D/W

PREVIOUS PAGES: A bold color
defines the open kitchen area. The
stainless steel base under the bar
is used for storage.
RIGHT: A hallway connects the two
studio apartments. A media niche
was created in the space formerly
used as a sleeping alcove.

LEFT: Leftover spaces in the master bathroom were converted into storage. Stone tile was used throughout to visually unify the space.
RIGHT: In the bedroom, the architect designed the bed and shelving.

PERIOD APARTMENT

ARCHITECT IAIN CAMPBELL DESIGN • **PHOTOGRAPHER** CHRISTOPHER CAMPBELL

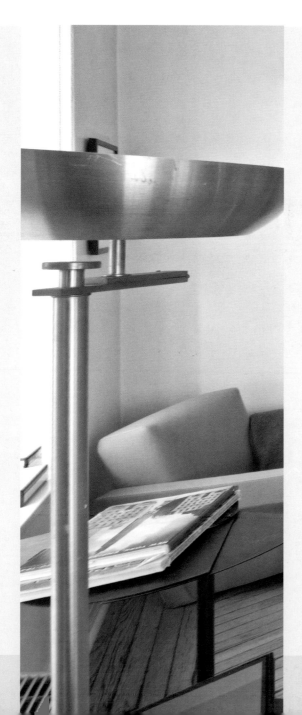

This studio apartment benefits from a thoughtful original layout and a corner location with good light and views. The owner decorated this pied-a-terre with furniture and objects of modern design, much of which would have been in production and available within a few years of the building's completion in 1931.

The living space converts to a bedroom instantly with a lateral fold-down bed, in the location of the original Murphy bed. The lateral bed allows a better use of space, including storage above. Smaller scaled furniture is up on legs to preserve an open, airy feel.

The original small kitchen was too narrow to allow counter on both long sides so the architect closed the original doorway and opened the kitchen to the living room, creating a highly functional "U" shape. In order to have a full complement of appliances, a cabinet-depth refrigerator was installed as well as an 18-inch dishwasher with cabinetry panels and an enameled 24-inch stove. Custom cabinetry maximizes the usable space with a corner cabinet and a pantry with a sliding, frosted-glass door. Custom stainless steel shelves allow for a display of the owner's dishes and collections. Forbo sheet linoleum floor, white honed statuary marble counters, and subway tile balance the modern and vintage elements of the apartment.

The original bath layout was preserved, using the original floor, refurbished recessed metal cabinets and the deep, original tub.

Existing Floor Plan

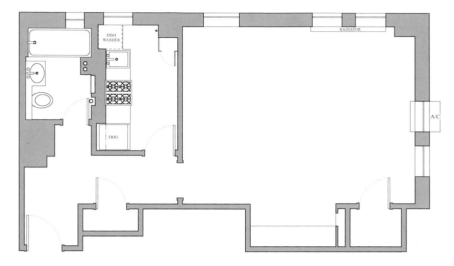

DISH
WASHER

RADIATOR

A/C

FRIG

New Floor Plan

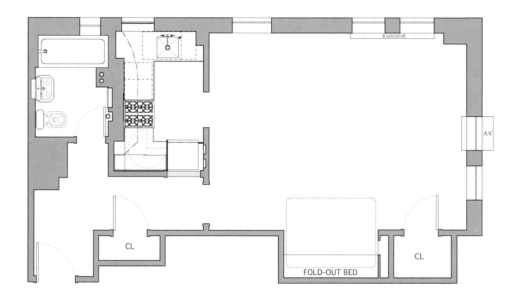

RADIATOR

A/C

CL

CL

FOLD-OUT BED

PREVIOUS PAGES: Much of the original
detail of the apartment was preserved.
The kitchen was reconfigured and
opened to the living area in the new
plan, creating more usable space.
RIGHT: Smaller scaled appliances and
custom cabinetry resulted in a very
efficient arrangement.
FAR RIGHT: The original bathroom was
augmented by new white subway tiles.

LEFT AND ABOVE: A view of the living room with the lateral folding bed in the up position and in the open, sleeping position.

WESTSIDE APARTMENT

690 SQUARE FEET

ARCHITECT IAIN CAMPBELL DESIGN • **PHOTOGRAPHER** CHRISTOPHER CAMPBELL

The owner/architect renovated this compact two-bedroom apartment himself, designing and building custom cabinetry and furniture, and frequenting local flea markets for vintage pieces to meet a wide variety of specific uses in a small space. The apartment has seven large windows and original chestnut moldings, hidden under layers of paint.

The living room functions as a quiet place to read, a place for social gathering, and as an additional guest room with a fold-out bed concealed in the custom designed sofa. The dining room does double duty as well as a library and office. Oak, bifold doors allow the living room to be closed off when the living room is used as a bedroom.

The master bedroom features custom built furniture and millwork, all designed by the owner, including the bed. The guest bedroom features an owner designed storage bed, an original chestnut closet, and adjustable shelving for storage.

In the kitchen, old growth cherry boards were used to build kitchen cabinet doors and drawer fronts. The revised layout allowed workspace on either side of the stove and for the deep refrigerator and newly-added washer and dryer to be better concealed. Deep drawers were chosen over lower cabinets, for their ease of access

The bathroom was rebuilt, using new tile and vintage fixtures including the original tub. The use of a corner sink and a tank toilet allowed for a more gracious layout.

Floor Plan

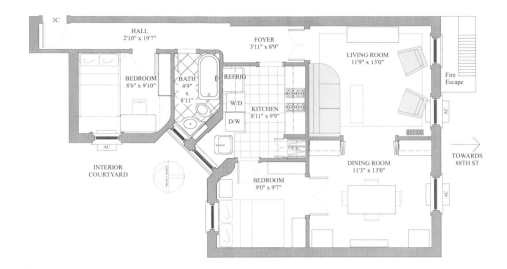

3C

HALL
2'10" x 19'7"

FOYER
3'11" x 8'9"

LIVING ROOM
11'9" x 13'0"

Fire
Escape

BEDROOM
8'6" x 9'10"

BATH
4'9"
x
8'11"

REFRIG

W/D

KITCHEN
8'11" x 9'9"

D/W

AC

AC

INTERIOR
COURTYARD

DINING ROOM
11'3" x 13'0"

TOWARDS
88TH ST

BEDROOM
9'0" x 9'7"

AC

PREVIOUS PAGES: The living room also serves as an extra guest room. Folding oak doors close to provide privacy from the dining area.
BELOW: Window grates are based on a Prairie Style design.
RIGHT: A view of the entry foyer with original chestnut moldings.

ABOVE: The folding oak doors are the same width as the dining room cabinets so that they do not appear to protrude into the room.
LEFT: The dining table was custom designed by the owner. The painting is by the owner's brother, Christopher Campbell.

LEFT: The renovated kitchen includes cabinetry made from old growth cherry boards.

LEFT: The guest bedroom features furniture designed by the architect/owner, including the storage bed.
ABOVE: A corner pedestal sink and a tank toilet make the small bathroom appear more spacious.

ABOVE: The master bedroom
features custom built furniture
and millwork.

DAYDREAMS

ARCHITECT OFFICE PARK • **PHOTOGRAPHERS** FLORIAN HOLZHERR, KRISTA NINIVAGGI

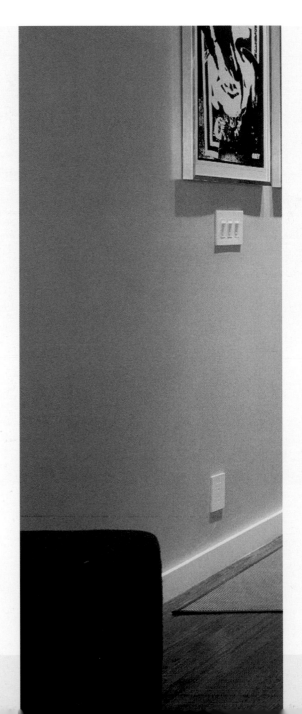

The two architect/owners rented this apartment for two years before convincing the owner to sell it to them, During that time they spent many hours daydreaming about how they would renovate the narrow 40-by-10-foot space. Prior to renovation, there were only two windows at one end of the apartment. Once they began ripping down the multiple layers of plaster and wall board, they discovered two windows that had been boarded up years ago. This major discovery brought needed light and air into the kitchen and bathroom areas.

In the new layout, the bedroom was located at the front of the apartment, and rests on a 14-inch-high platform, separated from the living area with floor-to-ceiling sliding translucent partitions. The bedroom was given a minimal amount of space so that the adjacent living area could be larger. Beneath the bedroom platform are three nine-foot-long drawers that provide additional storage. A fourth drawer slides out into the living area to become a guest bed.

At the other end of the narrow apartment is an open kitchen and then a dressing area with closets that leads to the bathroom. The galley kitchen, while compact, has a full complement of appliances and ample counter space for the couple, who enjoy cooking.

To further conserve space, pocket doors were used throughout the apartment. To gain additional storage, the owners took advantage of the high, nine and one-half-foot ceilings by adding overhead "attic" storage cabinets above the entry, kitchen, and shower, gaining over 24 cubic feet of storage for luggage and out-of-season clothing.

Floor Plan

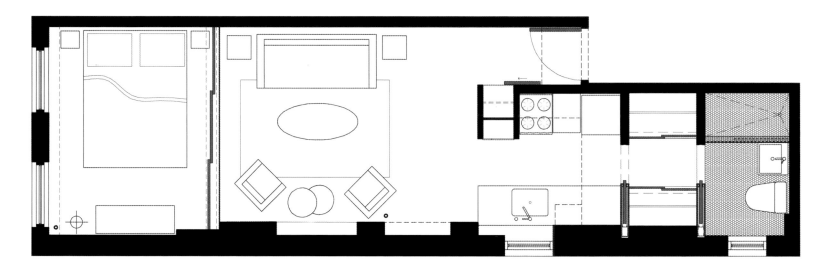

Elevation

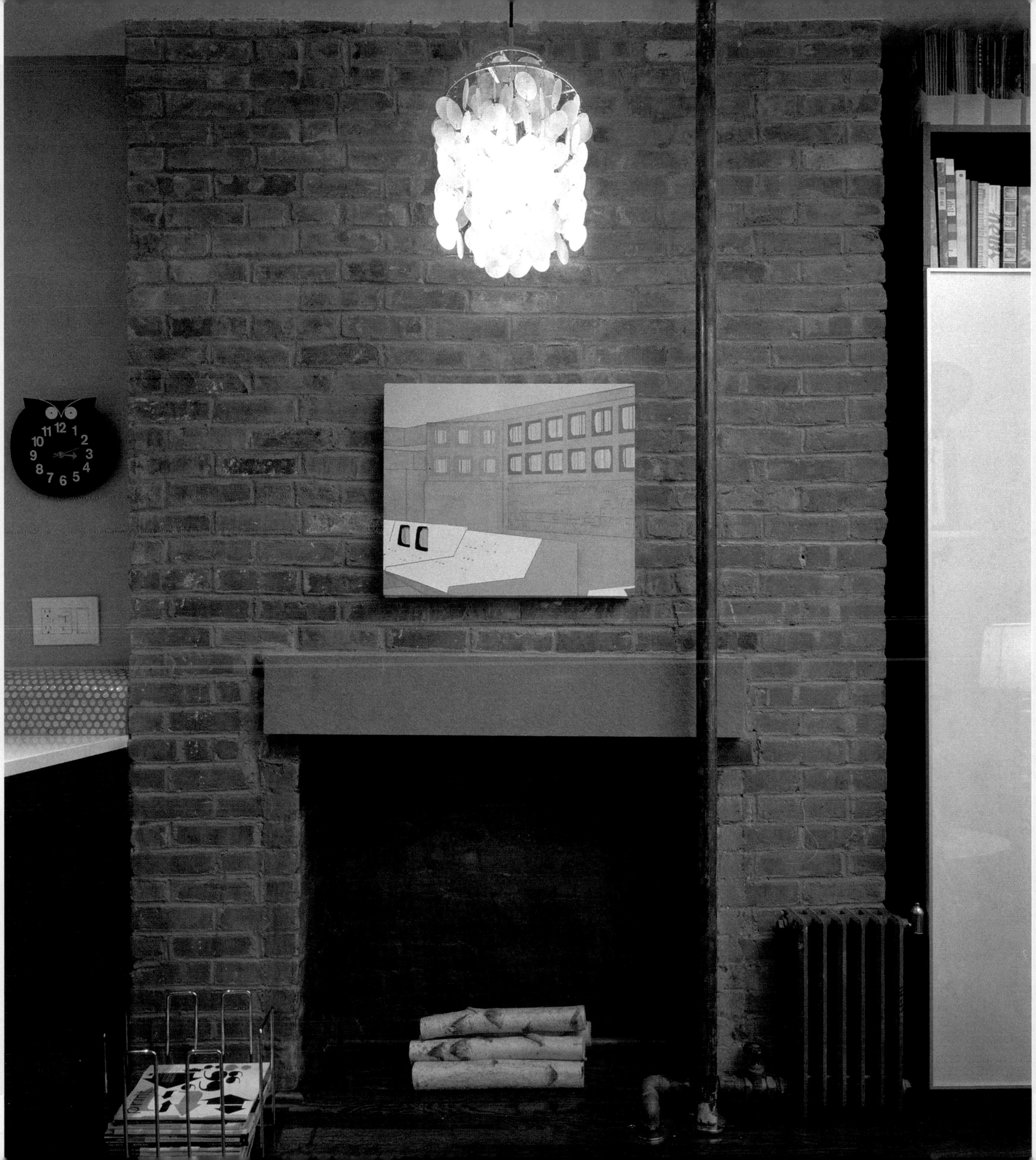

LEFT: A view of the living area separated from the bedroom by sliding translucent panels.

RIGHT: The bedroom floor was raised 14 inches to accommodate storage drawers beneath. One of these drawers becomes the guest bed and is shown here in the open position. The translucent panels provide privacy between the two sleeping areas.

LEFT: Beyond the translucent panels is the small bedroom, which enjoys light from the apartment's two principal windows.

RIGHT: The narrow four and one-half-foot-wide bathroom is made more functional by the use of a pocket entry door. Storage was created above the shower stall.

TRIBECA LOFT

1000 SQUARE FEET

ARCHITECT RB ARCHITECTS • **PHOTOGRAPHER** JAMES WILKINS

In an effort to create a social/entertaining area, a kitchen, a new master bedroom and bath, and a study/guest room, the architect chose to divide the existing open space with a full height closet that bisects the apartment, separating the public and private areas. The closet is accessible from both sides and is fitted with translucent glass doors and with glass panels at each side, maximizing natural light. The study and guest room is entered via full height sliding glass doors that, when opened, make the space part of the living area, or, when closed, provide privacy for a guest or for work.

The social areas include the open living room, with built-in custom cabinetry, including fireplace enclosure and a large freestanding desk. At one end is a custom dining table that separates the living area from the kitchen area.

The palette of materials chosen for this apartment—bamboo flooring, maple veneer cabinetry, black granite, and acid etched glass and aluminum for the doors—was deliberately limited in order to provide a consistency that would unify the spaces and produce a smooth visual flow.

Floor Plan

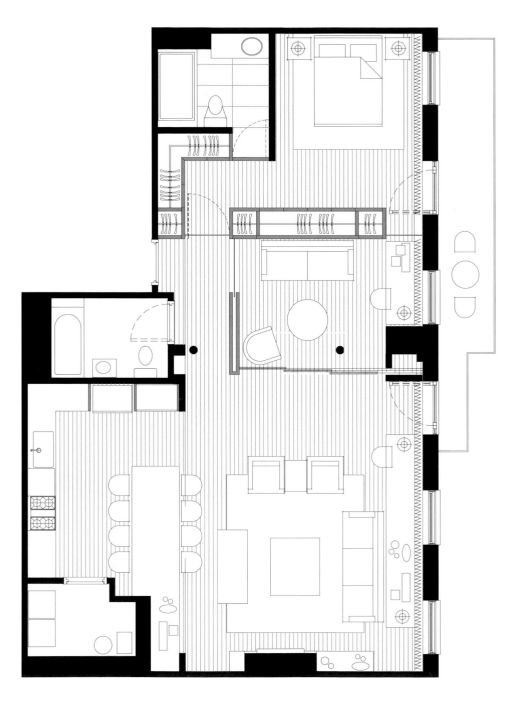

PREVIOUS PAGES: The living room features a built-in desk and bookcases. It is open to the kitchen, creating a large entertaining space.
BELOW: A view of the guest room from the living area with the sliding translucent doors. The door to the bedroom is to the left.
RIGHT: When the doors are open, the guest room becomes part of the living room.

LEFT: Maple veneer was used for the cabinetry.
ABOVE: The open kitchen is separated from the living room by the large custom table that also provides additional counter space for the kitchen.

CLEAN LINES

650 SQUARE FEET

ARCHITECT WEST CHIN ARCHITECT • **PHOTOGRAPHER** MIKIKO KIKUYAMA

Prior to renovation, this modest one-bedroom apartment, located in an old loft building in the West Village, had a small, dark kitchen and bathroom with an ill-conceived layout. The design concept for the new apartment was to create a light and airy, loft-like space, while providing a sense of privacy without visible clutter.

Achieving a separation between the public and private spaces in such a small space can be difficult without creating a sense of claustrophobia. The architect's solution was to insert a wooden box between the living room and the bedroom. The dark wood of the box appears to float within the white space of the apartment. Within the box at either end are sliding pocket doors. When drawn, the doors provide privacy for the bedroom and when retracted during the day, allow for an open circulation plan. Within the box is a television for each room, a computer desk, library, audiovisual equipment and a substantial amount of storage.

The open kitchen, while compact, has a full complement of appliances including a wine cooler. Corian was used for the counters and backsplash.

In addition to the storage provided by the box, the bedroom has a generous walk-in closet.

Floor Plan

bathroom

kitchen

dw below

refrigerator/ freezer

coat closet

books

closet

walk-in closet

linens

storage

av/storage

storage

storage

bedroom

living area

PREVIOUS PAGES: The box that divides the living room from the bedroom appears to float within the all white apartment. In the foreground is the kitchen with a built-in wine cooler.
BELOW LEFT: When the pocket doors that separate the living room from the bedroom are retracted, the space becomes more open and loft-like.
BELOW: A view from the living area to the bedroom through the open pocket door.

LEFT AND ABOVE: The open galley kitchen is in sharp contrast to the dark enclosed existing kitchen.

ABOVE: The floating box provides
provides privacy for the bedroom.

RIGHT: The bathroom features a custom tile weave wall with limestone floors.